940.4

HISTORY THROUGH
NeWspApErs

The Western Front in
WORLD WAR I

Paul Dowswell

Hodder
Wayland

an imprint of Hodder Children's Books

Produced for Hodder Wayland by
Discovery Books Ltd
Unit 3, 37 Watling Street, Leintwardine, Shropshire SY7 0LW

First published in 2002 by Hodder Wayland, an imprint of Hodder Children's Books

British Library Cataloguing in Publication Data
Dowswell, Paul
The Western Front in World War One. – (History through
newspapers)
1.World War, 1914-1918 – Campaigns – Western Front –
Sources – Juvenile literature 2.World War, 1914-1918 –
Campaigns – Western Front – Press coverage – Juvenile
literature
I.Title
940.4'144

ISBN 0750241837

Printed and bound in Italy by G. Canale & C.Sp.A, Turin

Designer: Ian Winton
Cover design: Claire Bond
Series editors: Jane Tyler and Kathryn Walker
Picture research: Rachel Tisdale

Learn.co.uk is a trade mark of Guardian Education Interactive Limited and is used under license

Hodder Children's Books would like to thank the following for the loan of their material:
Corbis: page 14/15; **Hulton Getty:** page 5, 6/7, 13, 17, 19, 20/21, 23, 24/25, 27, 29;
Mary Evans Picture Library: Cover, page 9, 11.

Hodder Children's Books would like to thank the following for permission to reproduce newspaper
articles: **by kind permission of Atlantic Syndication for Associated Newspapers:** page 8, 10,
22; © **Learnthings Limited and Guardian Newspapers Limited:** page 6, 12, 14, 20, 24, 30;
©News International Newspapers Limited 1915 and 1918: 16, 26.

Every effort has been made to contact copyright holders of any material reproduced in this book. Any
omissions will be rectified in subsequent printings if notice is given to the publishers.

The website addresses (URLs) included in this book were valid at the time of going to press. However,
because of the nature of the Internet, it is possible that some addresses may have changed, or sites
may have changed or closed down since publication. While the author and Publisher regret any
inconvenience this may cause readers, no responsibility for any such changes can be accepted by
either the author or the Publisher.

Hodder Children's Books
A division of Hodder Headline Limited
338 Euston Road
London NW1 3BH

CONTENTS

THE WESTERN FRONT

ABOUT THIS BOOK

This book presents a series of extracts from British newspapers published at the time of World War I. A range of newspapers has been used so that, to some limited extent, different opinions are represented. Each article deals with an important issue of the time. On the same double page you will find key background information and a separate 'Evaluation' panel which explains difficult points in the extract and suggests how to approach it as a piece of historical evidence. For example, it asks whether the statements in the extract are reliable and unbiased.

As newspapers appear daily or weekly, they deal with issues and events as they happen. To make money, they must sell in large numbers – which means that their contents must please their regular readers. So newspaper articles provide evidence about readers' opinions and attitudes.

Furthermore, each newspaper generally tries to attract particular groups of readers. It wants to please them, but also tries to keep or win their support for its policies. So a newspaper also tells us something about the ideas and aims of its owners and editors.

World War I, also known as the First World War, lasted for four terrible years. Between August 1914 and November 1918 troops from the continents of Europe, North America, Australasia and parts of Africa and Asia were engaged in a struggle for supremacy that would claim the lives of over nine million soldiers. The most intense area of fighting was a section of Europe stretching from the English Channel down to the Swiss border known as the '**Western Front**'. This is the area broadly covered by the newspaper reports in this book, and the '**theatre**' of warfare where British troops were most involved.

The war was fought in isolated spots throughout the globe, but the main battlefields were found in territory to both the west and east of Germany.

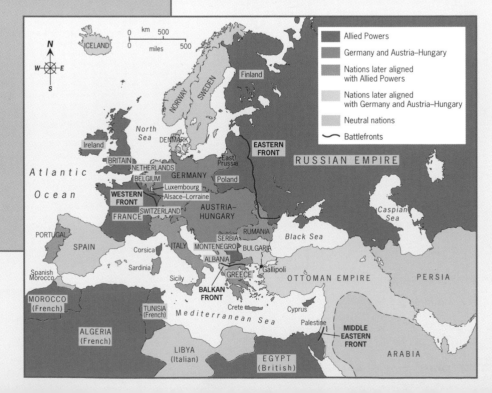

■	Allied Powers
■	Germany and Austria–Hungary
■	Nations later aligned with Allied Powers
■	Nations later aligned with Germany and Austria–Hungary
■	Neutral nations
⌒	Battlefronts

Although trenches guarded by barbed wire had been used in earlier conflicts, these muddy and uncomfortable fortifications became a symbol of World War I.

In 1914 people relied almost entirely on newspapers for news. There was no TV or radio broadcasting, although 'newsreels' – silent films of important events – were shown in cinemas. Today people are more inclined to doubt newspaper reports, but before and during the years of World War I, newspaper news was usually taken as fact. This gave newspaper owners and editors a great deal of power to shape public opinion. During the war Germany was depicted as a barbarous nation. Germans were commonly referred to as '**Huns**' – after a savage tribe of Eastern European warriors who plagued the Roman Empire in the 5th Century AD.

Censorship

One **media** historian, Philip Knightly, dismissed British newspapers of World War I thus: 'More deliberate lies were told than in any other period of history.' The era covered by this book is a shameful one for the British press. For example, the first day of the Battle of the Somme — the most disastrous bungle in British military history — was reported by *The Times* as 'a good day for England'. After the war *The Times* offered this excuse: 'The principal aim of the war policy of *The Times* was to increase the flow of **recruits**. It was an aim that would get little help from accounts of what happened to recruits once they became soldiers.'

Newspaper owners directed their journalists and editors to produce papers that would keep the **morale** of the British people high. But, even if the papers had had the inclination to report the carnage of the Western Front in realistic detail, they would have been unable to do so. War reporting was strictly controlled by an **Act** of Parliament passed on the outbreak of war called the Defence of the Realm Act (widely referred to as DORA). This law forbade publication of any information 'calculated to jeopardize [endanger] the success of the operations of any of His Majesty's forces, or assist the enemy'. In effect this meant that every war report had to be written in terms favourable to Britain.

DECLARING WAR ON GERMANY

Britain declared war on Germany on 4 August 1914, after the German army invaded Belgium. The Germans intended to sweep through this small, **neutral** country to capture Paris, the capital of France, which was Germany's most dangerous enemy. Britain, as an ally to France, immediately set about sending troops over to northern Europe to repel the German invasion. The initial strike force was called the British Expeditionary Force (known as the BEF). It was made up of units of the regular army and **reservists** (men who are not full-time soldiers but can be called up in times of emergency – known today as the Territorial Army). The report below concerns these reservists.

Your Country Needs You!

When fighting began, the British war minister, Lord Kitchener, issued a call for new **recruits**. The war was such a popular cause that thousands of men flocked to recruiting stations, creating a crisis in the army, which could not supply or accommodate such a vast new intake. These new recruits came to be known as 'Kitchener's army'.

WITH THE GUNS

The Reservists were leaving for London by the nine o' clock train. They were young men, some of them drunk. There was one bawling and brawling before the ticket window; there were two swaying on the steps of the subway shouting … One woman stood before the carriage window. She and her sweetheart were being very matter-of-fact, cheerful, and bumptious [self-important] over the parting. 'Well, so-long!' she cried as the train began to move. 'When you see 'em let 'em have it.'

'Ay, no fear,' shouted the man, and the train was gone, the man grinning. I thought what it would really be like, 'when he saw 'em.'

Last autumn I followed the Bavarian army down the Isar valley and near the foot of the Alps. Then I could see what war would be like – an affair entirely of machines, with men attached to the machines … It is a war of **artillery**, a war of machines, and men no more than the subjective material of [a part of] the machine. It is so unnatural as to be unthinkable. Yet we must think of it.

(*Above*) **This news item in the *Manchester Guardian* of 18 August 1914, describes British soldiers leaving to fight in France.**

Evaluation

Up until the outbreak of war the *Manchester Guardian* (now published as the *Guardian*), which was one of Britain's more liberal, radical newspapers, had been a firm opponent of any involvement of Britain in a European conflict. But once war broke out, the paper, like all national newspapers regardless of their previous opinion, sided with the government. Even so, this unusually frank piece has an element of doubt. Boldly reporting that some British soldiers had actually been seen behaving badly in public (drunk and brawling), the writer goes on to express his concern about the nature of the war they would have to fight. Advances in military technology in the previous half century, particularly in the killing power of artillery, rifles and machine guns, had made warfare a much deadlier affair.

The men depicted in this report were almost certainly travelling to their deaths. Over the autumn, the BEF fought fierce battles to halt the advance of the German army at Mons and Ypres. By the end of November barely one in 20 of those British soldiers sent to fight this crucial early stage of the war were still alive.

The suspension dots [...] which appear in the newspaper articles used in this book indicate where portions of the original text have been omitted, and text in square brackets has been added to explain certain words, terms or references.

Britain had not been involved in a major European war since Napoleonic times a century before, and most people expected this forthcoming conflict to be quickly decided. War was seen as a glamorous and glorious affair, with great marches and mighty battles. This romantic view would soon evaporate in the muddy **trenches** of the **Western Front**.

The end of an era. An excited crowd gathers in London's Trafalgar Square to cheer the outbreak of the war in August 1914. No one expected a bloody and protracted conflict that would last for over four dreadful years.

GERMAN ATROCITIES

The German assault on France, through **neutral** Belgium to Paris, was a drastic tactic which the Germans justified to themselves as a desperate necessity. Germany also had to fight against Russia in the east. She was keen to win a quick victory in France, so she could then concentrate all her forces on defeating the Russians. The quickest way to do this, thought the German generals, was to invade their neutral neighbours and fight with ruthless determination. There was little regard for the lives of ordinary people caught in the path of their advancing army, and in the opening stage of the war at least 5,000 Belgian civilians were killed.

Fuelling Hatred

For the British newspapers, this was a heaven-sent opportunity to stir up hatred against Germany, and convince the British public they were fighting a just and honourable war against a barbaric foe. Completely untrue stories of deliberate German atrocities, such as the replacing of bells in church steeples with hanging nuns, and widespread rape and child murder were widely reported.

By the third week of September, when the article (left) was written, the northern French city of Rheims was under **siege**, and its historic cathedral (where France had once crowned its kings) was hit by German **shells**.

A Deliberate Crime

The excuse with which the German General Staff has disingenuously [dishonestly] attempted to offer for the wanton [unrestrained] and sacrilegious [disrespectful] bombardment of Rheims Cathedral will not for one moment impose upon [deceive] the civilized world. The deed is one which covers with fresh shame and horror the German name … The Germans wreck everything they could destroy. It is not from any military necessity or by any mistake that this glorious monument to the past … has been shattered. The accuracy of the modern **artillery** is so perfect that, unless the German gunners had of set purpose directed their projectiles [shells] against it, it must have escaped untouched. The evidence of our special correspondent, who witnessed the deed, is conclusive. The Germans turned their shells on the cathedral because they wished to destroy it in a passion of rage and brutality.

The smoking ruins of Rheims and Louvain and of a dozen French and Belgium cities, the murder of priests, women and children … these are unimpeachable [reliable] witnesses to the passion for evil which has possessed the soul of the German race and made it at once the enemy of God and scourge [cause of suffering] of man.

This editorial in the *Daily Mail* of 22 September 1914, reflects on the shelling of Rheims cathedral, and other German 'outrages'.

For the British press, this was yet another example of '**Hunnish**' behaviour, or 'frightfulness', as was said in a popular phrase of the time.

For the British papers such incidents were all valuable ammunition in their war to convince both the British people, and neutral countries such as the United States, that Germany was not a civilized nation.

This characteristically over-the-top British cartoon, by Edmund J Sullivan, is entitled *The Crucifixion of Belgium*. It shows the German Kaiser, Wilhelm II, callously sharing a smoke with one of his soldiers, as an angel child, representing Belgium, is subjected to an agonizing death.

Evaluation

This was a leader or editorial, an article expressing the newspaper's views. The tone of outrage leaves the reader in no doubt as to the *Daily Mail's* opinion of the Germans. Yet even in today's battlefields, high-technology laser-guided missiles can still miss their target, and cause civilian casualties. Therefore, the article's insistence that the destruction of the cathedral is deliberate because 'the accuracy of modern artillery is so perfect' is almost certainly intended to show the Germans in the worst possible light rather than to express a genuine belief.

Reports such as this continued throughout the war. The famous writer Rudyard Kipling, who regularly penned articles for British newspapers, once even declared: 'There are only two divisions on the world today – Human Beings and Germans.'

THE BOWMEN OF MONS

The first great British battle of the **Western Front** was fought in Belgium at Mons over 23 and 24 August 1914. The high number of casualties there gave some idea of how much the new weapons had changed the face of warfare, and were an awful warning of the carnage yet to come.

The article below is a fanciful piece of fiction, written by journalist Arthur Machen, who said of it 'The tale is mere and sheer invention: I made it all up out of my own head … .' It describes an event during the Battle at Mons when besieged British troops were attacked by a huge wave of German soldiers. In the thick of the fighting, a soldier says a prayer to Britain's **patron saint**, St George, who immediately comes to the rescue with a squad of bowmen – the ghosts of English archers who had won a famous victory against the French at Agincourt in 1415.

THE BOWMEN
By Arthur Machen

At this very moment they saw from their **trenches** that a tremendous host [army] was moving against their line … As far as they could see the German infantry [foot-soldiers] was pressing on against them, column upon column, a grey world of men, ten thousand of them as it appeared afterwards. There was no hope at all…

'World without end, Amen.' said one British soldier with some irrelevance as he took aim and fired. And then he remembered a restaurant in London … On all the plates in this restaurant there was printed a figure of St George in blue, with the motto, *Adsit Anglis Sanctus Georgius – May Saint George be Present Help to the English* … now as he fired … he muttered this pious motto.

The roar of the battle died down in his ears to a gentle murmur; instead of it … he heard, or seemed to hear, thousands shouting 'St George! St George!' And as the soldier heard these voices he saw before him, beyond the trench, a long line of shapes, with a shining about them. They were like men who drew the bow, and with another shout, their cloud of arrows flew singing and tingling through the air towards the German host.

The Making of a Myth

Not intended to be taken as a serious news story, it was seized upon by many of the *Evening News's* readers and became exaggerated in its telling. Soon a fully-blown myth swept the country about an angel (not mentioned in the story here) leading British troops to victory against the Germans.

The Angel of Mons became the most famous myth of the war, but other stories, such as one about the Germans using the corpses of their dead soldiers to make soap and candles were also widely believed.

This story of the bowmen of Mons appeared in the *London Evening News* of 29 September 1914.

Evaluation

The 'host' in this extract is the approaching German army. Although *The Bowmen* was written as a fictitious story, it appeared in the news pages of the *Evening News*, and perhaps this is why many who read it took it as a report of actual events. Arthur Machen was extremely distressed and embarrassed by the effect that his sentimental story had on the British people. Yet such was the wave of patriotism that swept through the country at the start of the war, it was commonly felt to be disloyal to suggest the story was untrue.

It is difficult to imagine newspaper readers believing such a story today. But the fact that such a transparently fictional tale was swallowed whole by many people gives us a curious insight into both the hysteria apparent in Britain at the start of the war, and the naïve belief in the content of newspapers by many of the population.

This illustration by Alfred Pearse, which appeared after Arthur Machen's story had gripped the imagination of British newspaper readers, feeds the myth of the 'Bowmen of Mons'. The pious soldier on the right leaves the viewer in no doubt that God is on the side of the British, rather than the Germans.

THE TRENCHES ARE SET UP

When the war erupted in August, 1914, everyone thought the outcome would be quickly decided. The German Kaiser, or emperor, told his soldiers they would be home 'before the leaves fall from the trees'. British soldiers weren't quite so optimistic, but there was an often-voiced belief that the war would be 'over by Christmas'. It was not to be.

When the German army clashed with its French and British opponents on its way to Paris, the war ground to a bloody standstill. Both sides then tried to **outflank** the other, racing south-east and north-west in a bid to get behind their enemy. To maintain the territory they held, opposing armies dug long lines of **trenches**, heavily fortified with machine gun nests and thickets of barbed wire (described in the article below as 'entanglements').

Life under shell fire

Our men have made themselves fairly comfortable in the trenches, in the numerous quarries cut out of the hillsides, and in the picturesque villages whose steep streets and red tiled roofs climb the slopes and peep out amid the green and russet of the woods.

In the firing line the men sleep and obtain shelter in the **dug-outs** [holes] they have hollowed or 'undercut' in the sides of the trenches. These refuges are slightly raised above the bottom of the trench, so as to remain dry in wet weather. The floor of the trench is also sloped for the purpose of drainage. Some trenches are provided with head cover, and others with overhead cover, the latter, of course, giving protection from the weather as well as from **shrapnel** balls and splinters of **shells**.

'Ritz Hotel'
Considerable ingenuity [skill] has been exercised in making the shelters. Amongst other favourites are the 'Hotel Cecil', the 'Ritz Hotel', 'Billet-doux', 'Hotel Rue Dormir' &c. [etc.] On the road barricades also are to be found boards bearing the notice 'This way to the **Prussians**'. Obstacles of every kind abound, and at night each side can hear the enemy driving in pickets [pointed stakes] for entanglements. In some places the obstacles constructed by both sides are so close together that some wag [joker] has suggested that each should provide working parties to perform these fatiguing duties alternately, since their work is now almost indistinguishable and serves the same purpose.

Deadlock

By November 1914 a line of such trenches stretched from the English Channel to the Swiss border. Warfare had never before been fought on such a grand scale. The space between the front lines, known as 'no-man's land', soon became a quagmire of shell holes. With their lethal machine guns and barbed wire, trenches were extremely effective barriers to an attacking army. Against them, opposing generals could send only infantrymen armed with rifles, and often weighed down with 30 kilograms (60lbs) or so of equipment.

This news item from the *Manchester Guardian* of 17 October 1914, describes some of the first British trenches.

The stage was set for a terrible stalemate, sorrowfully described by one German doctor as 'the suicide of nations'. In increasingly desperate attempts to break this **deadlock**, generals launched massive **offensives** that wasted the lives of millions of men.

This propaganda photograph showing a group of stoic 'Tommies' huddled around a bucket that contained their dinner, cannot hide the dreadful conditions of the trenches on the Western Front. The soldier on the right, smoking his pipe and reading a letter from home, is seemingly unconcerned by the squalor that surrounds him.

Evaluation

This officially sanctioned report was reproduced in the *Manchester Guardian* from a Press Bureau account issued by the army (the Press Bureau was a government office which supplied stories to newspapers). By painting a picture of the 'picturesque villages' the writer attempts to make light of the squalid conditions men endured in the trenches, which were especially uncomfortable in the rainy autumn now upon them, and the winter months ahead.

The 'humorous' names given to squalid muddy dug-outs, often no more than holes in the side of the trench, are intended to convey an image of British 'pluck' and determination, and reassure readers who have sons and husbands in the **front line** that **morale** is high. But reading between the lines it is all to easy to see that the dual torments of bad weather and frequent bombardment ('from shrapnel balls and splinters of shells') would be a constant companion to the men in the trenches.

GAS ATTACK

Several new weapons appeared for the first time in World War I, including fighter and bomber aeroplanes, tanks and submarines. Gas was another innovation, and became one of the most unpleasant and widely used weapons of the war. Gas was undoubtedly effective, as the report below shows. At first, soldiers were told the best defence against gas was to urinate into a handkerchief and then breathe through it. But once all **front line** troops had been issued with gas masks, the new weapon became less effective.

Effects of Gas

Gas was first used by the Germans against the Russians on the **Eastern Front** then, shortly afterwards, on the **Western Front**. But even the most potent forms of gas usually disabled soldiers rather than killed them, crippling lungs and causing blisters on exposed skin. One legacy of the war was thousands of men disabled by their exposure to this chemical weapon, who would slowly die of **respiratory ailments**.

GERMAN GAS ENGINE IN ACTION

Largely by the use of a new and dangerous device, the Germans obtained a considerable success on Thursday evening in an attack on a large scale on the French position north of Ypres in the direction of Yser. Late last night the following report from Sir John French was issued by the Press Bureau: –

1. Yesterday evening the enemy developed an attack on the French troops on our left in the neighbourhood of Bixschoote and Langemarck on the north of the Ypres **salient**.

The attack was preceded by a heavy bombardment, the enemy at the same time making use of a large number of appliances for the production of asphyxiating [suffocating] gas.

The quantity produced indicates a long and deliberate preparation for the employment [use] of devices contrary to the terms of the Hague Convention, to which the enemy subscribed [agreed].

The false statements made by the Germans a week ago to the effect that we were using such gases is now explained. It was obviously an effort to diminish **neutral** criticism [lessen criticism from neutral countries] in advance.

2. During the night the French had to retire from the gas zone. Overwhelmed by the fumes, they have fallen back to the canal in the neighbourhood of Boesinghe.

Our front remains intact except on the extreme left, where the troops have had to readjust their line in order to conform with the new French line.

(*Left*) This news article from the *Manchester Guardian* of 24 April 1915 reports the first use of gas on the Western Front.

Evaluation

This typically critical piece, based almost word for word on an official Press Bureau report direct from the British army commander in France, Sir John French, affects shock at the German use of this new weapon. Interestingly, the article here even hints at German success, reporting French and British troops having 'fallen back', 'readjusted their line' and 'had to retire' — all gentler ways of admitting the soldiers are in retreat.

The Hague Convention, mentioned here, was a **treaty** signed by European countries including Germany and Britain, concerning the conduct of war. The piece goes on to mention how German reports a week previously had claimed the **Allies** were using gas, which was then untrue. Throughout the war all sides went to considerable lengths to persuade potential future allies, especially the USA (many of whose citizens were of German descent), that they were a worthy side to back. The article here makes it plain that it was the Germans who were the first nation to use gas.

Gas was a clumsy instrument of war. Initially released from huge canisters when the wind blew towards enemy **trenches**, it could all too easily blow back over the men who had sent it. **Shells** carrying gas were quickly developed, and proved to be more effective. When it was first used the British press were quick to dismiss gas as a 'typically **Hunnish**' weapon, and this newspaper report makes this disapproval obvious. But, despite this, gas was soon being used by all sides in the conflict.

The pitiful photograph shows soldiers who have been blinded by a German gas attack. They are forced to hold on to the man in front so as not to lose their way as they await medical treatment. Some of the soldiers have wet cloth pressed against their stinging eyes, but many have not even been provided with this minimal comfort.

THE SHELL SHORTAGE

Artillery shaped the face of World War I. The deep craters of no-man's land, and the muddy, churned-up terrain around the **front line**, with trunks of branchless trees and the remains of shell-blasted buildings, were all due to its awesome power. No other weapon killed more men in the war. Initially, artillery was seen as a solution to the **deadlock** of trench warfare. It was thought that a sufficiently powerful and thorough bombardment of the enemy's front line before an attack would destroy both its **trenches** and the barbed wire that lay before them (referred to in the article below as 'entanglements'). But in early 1915, the British army was hampered by a shortage of **shells**, also known as munitions. This is why the article here makes the case for more shells so forcefully.

NEED FOR SHELLS

BRITISH ATTACKS CHECKED
LIMITED SUPPLY THE CAUSE
A LESSON FROM FRANCE

LACK OF HIGH EXPLOSIVES

The result of our attacks on Saturday last in the districts of Fromelles and Richebourg were disappointing. We found the enemy much more strongly posted than we expected. We had not sufficiently high explosives to level [flatten] his **parapets** to the ground after the French practice, and when our infantry gallantly stormed the trenches, as they did in both attacks, they found a **garrison** undismayed, many entanglements still intact, and Maxims [a type of machine gun used by the Germans] on all sides ready to pour in streams of bullets. We could not maintain [defend] ourselves in the trenches won, and our reserves were not thrown in because the conditions for success in an assault were not present.

The attacks were well planned and valiantly conducted. The infantry did splendidly, but the conditions were too hard. The want [lack] of an unlimited supply of high explosives was a fatal bar to our success.

If we can break through this hard outer crust of the German defences, we believe that we can scatter the German Armies, whose **offensive** causes us no concern at all. But to break this hard crust we need more high explosives, more heavy howitzers [a type of artillery], and more men. This special form of warfare has no precedent [previous example] in history.

It is certain that we can smash the German crust if we have the means. So the means we must have, and as quickly as possible.

Increasing Production

Reports such as this one forced the government to act. The need for extra munitions led to great changes in the workforce, as women joined men in new munitions factories, and other places of employment. For the first time, in their hundreds of thousands, women earned a wage that would provide them with financial independence from family or husband.

The Times of 14 May 1915 reports on the munitions shortage.

But despite the increase in shell production that followed, artillery never lived up to its promise. During heavy bombardment, soldiers sheltered in underground **dug-outs**, and the high explosive impact of a shell was smothered by earth and mud. Barbed wire too, caught in the blast of a shell, would fly into the air but then fall back into place, virtually undamaged.

A British artillery bombardment in progress during the Battle of the Somme, over the summer of 1916. Some artillery bombardments on the Western Front were so massive they could even be heard in the South of England.

Evaluation

Despite its respectful tone, this article is a clear criticism of the British government, and its provision of munitions to the front line. In an era when the British press supported the war almost unthinkingly, this was highly unusual. The article was part of a carefully thought out campaign by General French, the Commander-in-Chief of British forces in France. He talked to *The Times'* military correspondent, Colonel Charles Reppington, and the paper's owner, Lord Northcliffe, about the shortage of shells.

During the early part of the 20th century, *The Times* was read by the country's most influential and important people. When Reppington's piece appeared, it caused a sensation. The problem was debated in Parliament, and lead to the fall of Herbert Asquith's Liberal Government and the formation of a new **coalition** government, under Asquith's leadership. A Minister of Munitions was appointed, and the job was given to David Lloyd George, who would succeed Asquith in 1916 as Britain's wartime leader.

CONSCRIPTION

When war broke out British people flocked to join the armed forces in their hundreds of thousands. Between August 1914 and January 1916, two and a half million men signed up, to make what was then the largest volunteer army in history. But after a year and a half, the flow of new **recruits** had slowed to a trickle. British generals were convinced that the way out of the trench **deadlock** of the **Western Front** was 'a big push' – a massive attack that would sweep the enemy aside through sheer force of numbers. For this they needed the 'great army' the headline below mentions.

At the start of the war conscription (compulsory service in the armed forces) had been ruled out, on the grounds that it would be too unpopular. But as the war dragged on it became more and more apparent that the military needed every man it could get. Lord Kitchener's appeal here succeeded. Conscription was introduced in March 1916.

LORD KITCHENER TELLS SHIRKERS WHY THEY ARE TO BE FETCHED

GREAT ARMY NEEDED TO SECURE VICTORY

In a short and interesting speech, Lord Kitchener in the House of Lords last night gave his views on the need for more men and the inadequacy of the voluntary system.

'In the early stages of the war men responded to the call in almost embarrassing thousands, and until a few months ago maintained, by a steady flow of recruits, the supply of men we required in as large numbers as we could train and equip.

'The cadres [military units] of the large Army we now possess having been formed, it is necessary to keep it up to strength in the field by a constant supply of reserves replenishing the wastage of war.

'It only affects, during the period of the war, one class of men, among whom there are undoubtedly a certain number who have but a poor idea of their duties as citizens, and require some persuasion greater than appeal to bring them to the colours [British flag].

'We are now asking parliament to sanction [authorize] a change, as it has been proved that, in the special circumstances of this utterly unprecedented struggle, the existing system without modification is not equal to maintaining the Army which is needed to secure victory.'

Objectors

However, the rights of those opposed to fighting on political or religious grounds were partially recognized. Such men, known as 'conscientious objectors', and more popularly as 'conchies', faced great ridicule and hostility from the general population. Some of the 16,500 men who were classed as conscientious objectors volunteered for medical or agricultural work, but those who refused to take part in any activity which helped Britain in the war were imprisoned for their beliefs.

The *Daily Mirror* of 6 January 1916 reports Lord Kitchener's speech to the House of Lords.

Evaluation

Lord Kitchener was the British Secretary of State for War. His speech here is reported plainly, with no comment from the newspaper itself, aside from the headline, which, with its harsh reference to 'shirkers', plainly states the *Daily Mirror's* attitude towards men who had not volunteered for the armed forces. Kitchener too, speaks unsympathetically of those with 'a poor idea of their duties as citizens' who 'require some persuasion greater than appeal to bring them to the colours' – meaning the national flag, – a symbol of Britain.

During the war the terrible extent of casualties was never directly referred to in the newspapers. Yet, even here, between the lines, the more perceptive reader would wonder what had happened to the men who had 'responded to the call in almost embarrassing thousands', who now needed to be replaced. Their fate is hinted at in the throwaway phrase 'the wastage of war'.

A recruitment poster showing a painting of the British Secretary of State for War, Lord Kitchener. Cleverly designed so that the finger and eyes would seem to follow the viewer as he walked past, this poster remains one of the most famous and lasting images of the war.

BATTLE OF THE SOMME

Today the Battle of the Somme has come to symbolize all that was wrong with the British campaign on the **Western Front**, and the first day, reported in the article below, is still the most disastrous day's casualty figure in British military history. After a week-long bombardment of the enemy front lines with one and a half million **shells**, 120,000 men advanced towards the German **trenches**, starting at 7.30 am on Saturday, 1 July 1916. The Germans, well protected in deep **dug-outs**, emerged virtually unscathed as soon as the shelling stopped, to man their machine guns. The carnage was pitiful. In the first hour alone, thousands of British troops, advancing in waves of straight lines, as they had been trained to do, were mown down like sheaves of corn. By early afternoon the battle had been lost, but it would carry on for another dreadful five months.

BRITISH FRENCH BLOW

After the stupendous bombardment of the past week the British and French launched on Saturday morning a great attack on both sides of the River Somme. The battle-front extended over 20 miles [32 kilometres] north of the river and about four miles [6.5 kilometres] south of it …

Most success was gained by the British and French along the southern half of the line, where advances of 1,000 to 2,000 yards [900 to 1,800 metres] were made and a number of villages captured. Up to the official reports of last night the number of prisoners recorded was over 3,500 taken by the British, and over 6,000 taken by the French.

Progress was continued yesterday. The British took Fricourt and ground to the east of the village, and despite stubborn resistance by the enemy at points further north our head-quarters last night described the general situation as favourable and the German losses greater than had at first been estimated. The French south of the Somme penetrated the German second line at some points. They have taken some gains.

This news article, from the *Manchester Guardian* of 3 July 1916, reports the opening of the Battle of the Somme two days earlier.

The Human Cost

At the end of the first day over 20,000 men had been killed, and another 40,000 had been wounded.

Many of these injured men still lay in no man's land, waiting for darkness to fall, in the hope that they could crawl back to their own line, or be picked up by a stretcher team without catching the attention of a German machine gunner. The campaign was finally called off in November 1916. During this time the **Allies** gained a few hundred metres of ground at the cost of over 600,000 British and French lives.

On the first day of the Battle of the Somme, British soldiers emerge from the relative safety of a trench to brave the barbed wire and withering machine gun fire of their German opponents.

Evaluation

Troops who survived such battles were disgusted by the reports they read in the papers about what had happened to them. No one would have guessed that the first day of the Battle of the Somme had been a disaster from articles such as this. All other British papers carried similar news.

The article goes on to quote from a 'semi-official review of the operation' which makes the following astonishing claim of the disastrous attack: 'The first day of the **offensive** is therefore very satisfactory … it is important above all because it is rich in promise … It is … a slow, continuous, and methodical push, sparing in lives…'

THE WAR OF ATTRITION

1916 had been a year of disasters. Sir John French, unable to find a solution to the stalemate of the **Western Front**, had resigned in December 1915. His replacement as Commander-in-Chief, Douglas Haig, had unleashed his army in the long promised 'big push' at the Somme, which ended in disastrous defeat. Britain's ally France suffered equally dreadful bloodshed at Verdun, where another 300,000 had been killed defending this French fortress from German attack. The conflict had become a war of attrition – where one side seeks to wear the other out, rather than hopes to win a decisive victory on the battlefield.

What Lay Ahead

The optimism of the article below is entirely unfounded. The new year of 1917 would bring even further disasters. Another British **offensive** at Passchendaele would cost 300,000 more lives. Massively successful German U-boat (submarine) attacks on cargo ships carrying vital food supplies to Britain would leave the country a mere six weeks away from starvation. Worst of all, Russia would surrender to Germany after a communist revolution there deposed the government. Germany, free from having to fight a war on both her western and eastern borders, was now able to concentrate all her strength on a great campaign in the west.

But there was good news too. In April 1917, America joined the war on the side of Britain and France. Although it would be another year before American soldiers arrived to fight on the Western Front, this at least was grounds for optimism.

1917
THE YEAR OF VICTORY

By Lovat Fraser

This is the third New Year's Day since Germany plunged the world into war. It dawns more hopefully for the **Allies** than any day since German cavalry rode across the French frontier at Cirey in the first hours of August 1914.

In the coming year our people must back up the men in the **trenches**. Are they doing it? One's final impression is that the civilian element falls short of complete fulfilment. The warm enthusiasm of two years ago has not yet been fully replaced by that dogged determination which has always been at the back of every British success in war.

Have we thrown our full weight into the war? Do we yet realize that the time has come when *every personal action should have for its object the winning of the war?*

The point which must strike all thoughtful men is the extreme urgency of the present situation. We must win now or not at all. Every man and woman of serviceable age who is not this spring doing something to assist the common object of winning the war must be enrolled. We cannot wait until another spring. It is now or never.

This article appeared in the *Daily Mail* of New Year's Day, 1917.

The remains of the French village of St Baussant. Many towns and villages unlucky enough to lie along the battlelines of the Western Front were reduced to a similar state.

Evaluation

Reading like a pep talk to a weary rugby team, Lovat Fraser's call to further effort and sacrifice almost certainly fell on hard ground, even among the *Daily Mail's* readership — a paper renowned for its intense patriotism. Other parts of the article not reproduced here search for a reason for Britain's failure to win the war — suggesting too great a concentration on other fronts, women at home not 'doing their bit', the government not pursuing the war vigorously enough. Yet, with hindsight, all seem to lack real substance, and show no recognition of the fact that the war was dragging on because there was no military solution to the **deadlock** of the trenches.

Fraser concluded his piece by saying 'We shall win in the west, and win quickly.' Even *The Times*, usually the government's staunchest supporter, did not agree with him. A similar article in that paper of the same day admitted that the war would drag on, and concluded; '…anything like a definite decision seems far distant.'

THE GERMAN OFFENSIVE OF 1918

Now freed from the two-front war that had divided their forces, the German army prepared its own attack on the **Allied** forces on the **Western Front** with the last of its dwindling strength. With a successful Allied navy **blockade** restricting the supply of food and other materials into Germany, and the imminent arrival of fresh American troops on the Western Front, this new **offensive** had a desperate 'do or die' quality to it. The results were impressive. The 'Ludendorff Offensive', named after the General who directed it, was launched in the third week of March 1918, and almost won the war.

This news report from the *Manchester Guardian* of 22 March 1918 concerns the German breakthrough on the Western Front.

STRUGGLE ON CAMBRAI SALIENT –

a Hurricane of Gas Shells

A German offensive against our front has opened … At about 5 o' clock this morning the enemy began an intense bombardment of our lines … After several hours of his hurricane shelling [very intense shelling], the German infantry advanced and developed attacks against a number of strategic points …

It is a menace which cannot be taken lightly, and at the present moment our troops are fighting not only for their own lives but also for the fate of England and all our race. During the last few weeks I have been along the sectors now involved in this battle, and have met the men who today are fighting to hold their lines against the enemy's storm troops under the fury of his fire. I have observed the spirit of these men of ours, their confidence, their splendid faith, their quiet and cheerful courage, their lack of worry until this hour should come, the curious incredulity [disbelief] they had that the enemy would dare to attack them because of the strength of their positions and of our great gunfire.

The heart of all the people of our race must go out to these battalions [military units] upon whom our destiny depends, and who now, while I write, are making a wall with their bodies against the evil and the power of our enemy.

New Tactics

Instead of the standard practice of sending line upon line of men against **trenches** bristling with machine guns, the Germans developed new offensive techniques, hinted at in the article below. Small groups of '**storm troopers**' made surprise attacks, probing the enemy's **front line** for weak spots. Then, when they had found them, reinforcements would break through. At first the attacks were a great success.

By early June the Germans had reached the River Marne, less than 100 kilometres [62 miles] from Paris, and a German victory looked possible. But in July, a French counter-attack broke the momentum of the offensive. An Allied **counter-offensive** of August that year was the beginning of the end. Within a hundred days German troops had been forced back to their own border.

German troops advance past a defensive barricade and into the French town of Bailleul, during the great German offensive of the spring of 1918. They have just driven British troops from the town.

THE ARRIVAL OF US TROOPS

The United States finally joined World War I in April 1917. This was mainly due to Germany's decision in February 1917 to relaunch submarine attacks on any vessels sailing to Britain or France, regardless of whether or not the vessel was from a **neutral** country. (The Germans had suspended such actions in 1915, for fear of bringing America into the war on the side of the **Allies**.) Sure enough, the American government found such a tactic unacceptable, as it directly affected their cargo ships and passenger liners to Europe.

Before American troops could be committed to battle an army had to be prepared. Fewer than 73,000 Americans volunteered to fight when war broke out, so conscription was immediately introduced to raise America's armed forces to fighting strength. Men had to be trained and transported from North America to Europe, which took the best part of a year. US units first went into action in large numbers in April 1918, as reported in this news item. Their arrival was a huge blessing to the French and British armies, who had just fought off the Ludendorff **Offensive**, and were in an exhausted and depleted state.

US TROOPS' STIFFEST FIGHT. GEN. PERSHING'S REPORT

(From our correspondent) New York, 23 April

The American Press is filled with satisfaction at the manner in which General Pershing's troops on Saturday sustained and repelled the severest attack yet made against them by the Germans. General Pershing's report says: —
'The losses sustained by us were no larger than could in reason have been expected. The engagement was the most severe in which Americans have taken part ...'

The special correspondent of the *New York Sun* illustrates the spirit of the American soldiers by quoting the remarks of a young trooper who was in the thick of the fight and is now in hospital suffering from **shrapnel** wounds.
'Tell them at home' (said this lad) 'that we are just beginning. It was time to see our men go at the **Huns**. All of us who thought baseball was a great American game have changed our minds. There is only one game to keep the American flag flying — that is, to kill Huns. I got several before they got me.'

US Impact

American troops fought with great determination and success. That summer an **Allied** offensive was launched against the German army. The addition of American soldiers, and the new, highly effective tank, made this final 'big push' a success. By early November, Germany's shattered armies had been pushed back to their own borders, and Germany called for a halt in the fighting.

This news item appeared in *The Times*, on 24 April 1918.

Following an intense period of training, these American soldiers have been packed aboard an ocean-going liner and are travelling to France. Fresh troops such as these were an invaluable help to the exhausted British and French armies.

Evaluation

This article in *The Times* was intended to show its readers how news of the war was being reported in the United States. It is interesting to note that official news from the American army is written in the same reassuring but utterly meaningless tone as that of the British — 'losses sustained by us were no larger than could in reason be expected'. Is that low or high? The reader will never know. The quote from the soldier has almost certainly been made up by the journalist — it sounds much too slick and knowing to have come from the lips of a wounded and low ranking soldier. 'I got several before they got me,' sounds like something from a newspaper strip cartoon.

THE END OF THE WAR

World War I ended when **Allied** troops reached the German border. At this point, the German government called for an armistice (ceasefire) rather than surrender. News of the ceasefire, at 11.00 am on 11 November 1918, was greeted with hysteria in the capitals of the victors, but the troops on the **front line** were more subdued. One colonel who wrote an account of that day recorded that fighting had gone on almost to the last moment. He reflected: 'The match was over; it had been a damn bad game.'

Effects on Germany

Germany's population were deeply shocked by the armistice. Their own newspapers led them to believe they were winning the war. But Germany was at the point of collapse. Food and fuel shortages had led to great unrest among the civilian population, and the German government feared a communist revolution. Germany's **allies**, Austria-Hungary, Bulgaria and Turkey were also near to collapse, and in late October a **mutiny** occurred in the German fleet.

As well as the fear of a communist revolution, Germany hoped that a ceasefire would prevent the country being occupied by Allied troops. But the peace **treaty** that followed, negotiated at Versailles, France, between January and June 1919, was a disaster for Germany. Large areas of her territory were given to other nations, Germany was made to accept responsibility for the war and pay reparations (compensation) to the victors, and her armed forces were subjected to strict limits in size. The treaty caused such bitterness that it led to the rise of Hitler and the Nazis, which in turn led directly to World War II.

How the Great News Was Received

People everywhere rushed into the streets from house, factory, and workshop and children helter-skelter from the school crying 'The war is over'. In a few minutes the little boys in red with the bugles, who used to send us to bed when the Gothas [German bombers] had gone, were starting out blowing the cheery 'All clear' for the war. These chubby little angels of goodwill were greeted everywhere with affectionate laughter as they blew away the four years' nightmare and all its horrors. The trains on all the lines carried on the note with a wheezy shriek of delight. The fat tugs on the river tried to play a tune on one note …

Looking from a Fleet Street window it was curious to see how instantaneous the swarm rushed out. The crowd gathered momentum in a most extraordinary way. Within ten minutes I saw on the hood of a bus over the drive an officer, a private, a **Wren**, and a **WAAC** dancing a peace dance. Nobody paid any fares — indeed very soon the conductresses gave up hope of collecting them. Motor cars in a steady stream came along, with people sticking to every inch of them like flies on treacle.

The *Manchester Guardian* of 12 November 1918 reports on public reaction to the armistice.

Evaluation

This sentimental report, based on the view from the window of the *Manchester Guardian's* central London office, gives a rather guarded impression of the wild celebrations that greeted the end of the war. The 'little boys in red' mentioned here, are part of London's air-raid warning system, against the German Gotha bombers that occasionally raided the capital.

Here the reporter affects mild shock and amusement at the fact that 'an officer (and) a private' are dancing together, and people are not paying their bus fares. In fact, there was a total breakdown of normal behaviour, as people free from 'the four years' nightmare and all its horrors' completely lost their inhibitions. Amid the wild celebrations complete strangers embraced passionately in the streets. In the repressive and more puritanical age of 1918 this was something even more unusual than it would be now.

Waving a combination of British and American flags, men and women, some civilian, some in uniform, celebrate the end of the war on the streets of London.

TIMELINE

1914:

3 August — Germany declares war on France and invades Belgium

4 August — Britain declares war on Germany

September — French army stops German advance at Battle of Marne

October/November — Trench systems established on Western Front

1915:

April 22 — First use of gas on Western Front, at Ypres

May — Shortage of shells for British artillery on Western Front causes press campaign in Britain which leads to fall of Liberal government

1916:

February 21 — Battle of Verdun between Germany and France begins (ends December)

March 1916 — Conscription introduced in Britain

July 1 — Battle of Somme between Britain and Germany begins (ends November)

September 15 — First use, by British, of tanks

1917:

April 6 — US declares war on Germany

May-June — Mutinies in French army

November 29 — Tanks used successfully at Battle of Cambrai

December 17 — Russia signs truce with Germany and withdraws from war

1918:

March 21 — German army launches final offensive on Western Front

April 24 — First use of American troops on Western Front

August 8 — Allies launch final offensive against German army, which leads to German defeat

November 11 — Armistice (truce) signed between Allies and Germany

GLOSSARY

ACT: An Act of Parliament — that is, a law made by Parliament.

ALLIES: The opponents of Germany, Austria-Hungary and Turkey – principally Britain, France, and their empires, Russia, and later the United States.

ARTILLERY: Large guns that fire explosive SHELLS.

BLOCKADE: Naval action that prevents ships from entering a foreign port or ports.

COALITION: Different political parties that join together to form a government.

COUNTER-OFFENSIVE: A series of attacks by an army, in response to an attack on itself.

DEADLOCK: Stalemate – a situation where two opposing forces are not strong enough to defeat each other.

DUG-OUTS: Holes dug into the ground or the side of a trench to provide shelter.

EASTERN FRONT: Main area of fighting in eastern Europe during World War I.

FRONT LINE: Area of a battlefield closest to the enemy

GARRISON: The troops defending a fort, town or other relatively small space.

HUNS: Name given to the Germans by the Allies, after a tribe of savage barbarians that threatened the Roman Empire (adjective **Hunnish**).

MEDIA: General word for newspapers, TV, films, radio and other forms of mass communications.

MORALE: The spirit of a person or group of people, for example, whether they feel enthusiastic or pessimistic about a particular course of action.

MUTINY: A situation in the armed forces where servicemen refuse to obey orders.

NEUTRAL: A country which does not support one side or another in a war.

OFFENSIVE: Large, preplanned attack.

OUTFLANK: To get behind an enemy army by going round the side of it.

PARAPET: A low wall built along the top of a trench to protect and hide troops.

PATRON SAINT: A saint regarded as the protector of a particular country or group of people.

PRUSSIANS: Literally, people from Prussia – a region of Germany. Prussia was supposedly famed for the ferocity and warlike attitude of its inhabitants.

RECRUITS: Young men who join the army (either voluntarily, or due to conscription).

RESERVISTS: Members of the army who are not full-time soldiers, but who can be called up in times of emergency.

RESPIRATORY AILMENTS: Illnesses that affect one's ability to breathe.

SALIENT: A part of an army's front line which projects forward into enemy territory.

SHELLS: Metal cases containing explosives or other harmful materials.

SHRAPNEL: Form of explosive that scatters small pieces of metal.

SIEGE: An offensive operation whereby a fortified enemy position is completely surrounded, to prevent the supply of food and ammunition and other essentials.

STORM TROOPERS: Troops who specialise in attacking enemy positions by moving forward in small well-armed groups.

THEATRE (OF WARFARE): Particular area of the world where opposing armies fight each other.

TREATY: Agreement reached between two countries.

TRENCHES: Lines of ditches fortified by sandbags and barbed wire, which soldiers dig to protect themselves and defend their positions.

WAAC: Women's Army Auxiliary Corps, or a member of the corps.

WESTERN FRONT: The main battleground in Western Europe, stretching from the Belgian coast to Switzerland.

WREN: Informal name for a woman who is in the WRNS – the Women's Royal Navy Service.

RESOURCES

Books

Steen, O, Hansen, *The War in the Trenches*, 2000, Hodder Wayland

Dowswell, P, *History Through Poetry – World War One*, 2001, Hodder Wayland

Dowswell, P, *Weapons and Technology of World War One*, 2002, Heinemann

Allan, T, *20th Century Perspectives – Causes of World War I*, 2002, Hodder Wayland

Brooman, J, *General Haig: Butcher or War Winner?*, 1998, Longman

Reynoldson, F, *Key Battles of World War One*, 2001, Heinemann

Websites

Recommended by the History Channel, this also has useful links to other sites:
http://www.pitt.edu/~pugachev/greatwar/ww1.html

The BBC site for the war:
www.bbc.co.uk/history/wwone.shtml

The site of Britain's Imperial War Museum, a major repository of World War I documents and artefacts:
www.iwm.org.uk/

Visit www.learn.co.uk, the award-winning educational website backed by the *Guardian*, for exciting historical resources and online events.

Places to visit

Imperial War Museum, London

Royal Air Force Museum, Duxford

Bovington Tank Museum, Dorset

INDEX